AF428501

For
Ay'deen
Kayden
Logan
Ryder
Saint
&
Wyitt

Be UNSTOPPABLE!

Work
work
work
work
work
work
work
WORK!

Its all Wally ever did.
He worked all day
from light to dark,
but he was just a little kid.

From the time he was
old enough to walk and talk,
Wally had to work.

Wally lived on a small farm
with his mom, Miss Courtney,
and his brothers and sisters.

They worked all the time, too,
and they never got any money, either.

The man who owned the small farm
also thought he owned Wally T
and his family.
Even Wally's mom, Miss Courtney.

This was a long
time ago.
There were a lot of people
who thought they could
OWN other people...

...and make them
work for free.

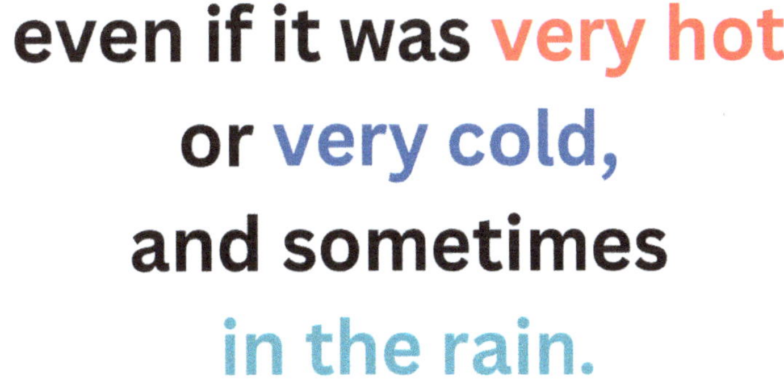

The hardworking people
had to work
all the time,

even if it was **very hot**
or **very cold**,
and sometimes
in the rain.

They couldn't
leave if they
wanted to go live
somewhere else.

None of this made sense to Wally T!

People own
all kinds of things
from blocks and pails
to fluffy dogs
with curly tails...
...but people
CANNOT
OWN
other people.

Wally stayed on the farm
with his family
until he was a big boy,
13 years old.

But then the man
who owned the farm
-and thought he owned Wally T-
took Wally away
from the farm
and away from his family.

Wally had to go live in a different place now.
He had to work for another man.

The new place was like a jail.
They kept hardworking people there,
even if they
didn't do anything bad.

Wally's job was to get the
hardworking people
cleaned up and ready,
so people could come
and buy them.

He still did not
get any money.

Wally stayed at the jail for a while.

Then a man with a bigger farm
came and paid for Wally T
and took him away.

They rode a train for 3 days.

Now Wally was even further away
from the small farm where he grew up.

Far far away from Miss Courtney.

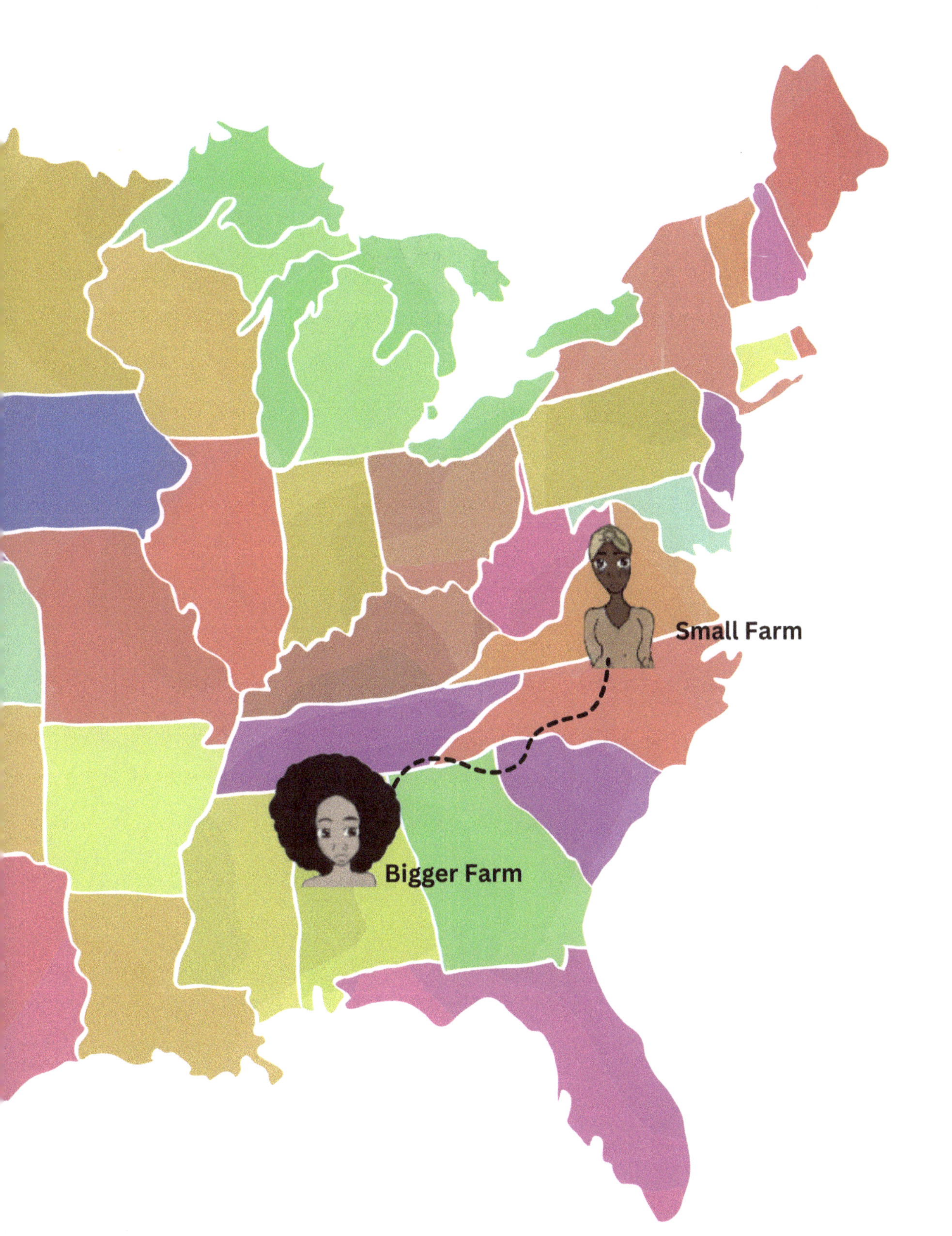

Small Farm
Bigger Farm

The Bigger Farm Man
made Wally T
and lots of other hardworking people
work all the time.

Planting and picking
and tending crops
and cooking
and cleaning
and sewing
and toting
and taking care of children
and taking care of grown-ups
and taking care of animals
and taking care of EVERYTHING else.

He never gave them any money.

If they didn't
do what he said,
he punished them.

And if they
tried to leave,
he punished them
for that, too.

Wally T didn't care.

He knew people
could not
own
other people.

So he left.

He wanted to find a way back
to the train and back to his mom.

The Bigger Farm Man sent
People Catchers
to find Wally T.

And they did.

They brought him back to the farm
and they hurt him.

They tried to make him scared
to run away again.

But Wally T wasn't scared
of being hurt.
He was scared
of being trapped.

So after a while, he left again.

And the man sent the People Catchers again.

And they found him
 and hurt him again.

Wally T stayed on the farm
for a while
and worked for a while,
but then he left
again.

And the same thing happened again.

When Wally T left for the fourth time,
he hid out.

Some people from a different farm
helped him.
They worked hard, too,
and they never got any money.
They couldn't leave their farm.
But they tried to help Wally T
get himself free.

They didn't have a lot of food,
but they shared the little bit they had,
and they tried to keep Wally safe.

After more than
100 days of hiding out,
the People Catchers
found Wally T
for the fourth time.

The Bigger Farm Man was sick of
trying to own Wally T!

He sold Wally to go live with another man,
a man who sold all kinds of things.

Now he lived super far away
from Miss Courtney.

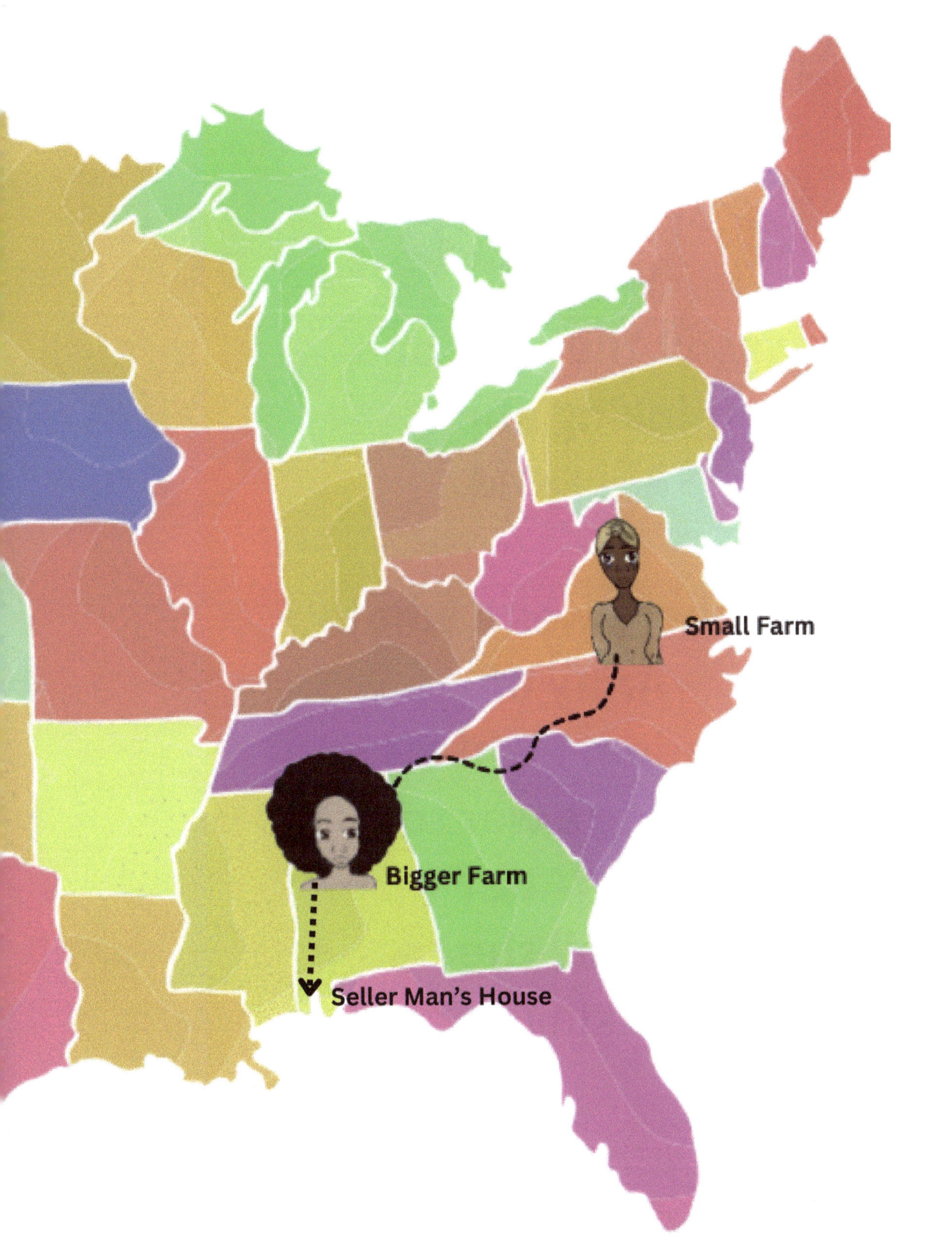

Small Farm
Bigger Farm
Seller Man's House

By this time,
Wally T
wasn't the only one
thinking about
FREEDOM.

Now there was a whole
Army of
Freedom Fighters
fighting a war to
FREE WALLY T
and all the
hardworking people.

Wally T was a young man now,
17 years old,
and he was smart.

The Seller Man decided to make
Wally T his carriage driver.

One day while Wally
was driving the carriage
on a busy street,
something scared the horse.

It jerked up onto its hind legs
and broke the harness.

Wally fell to the ground
and the carriage tipped over.
It was a busted mess!

Seller Man blamed Wally T
and paid a man to hurt him.
Then he told Wally
to walk back to his house.

Wally was used to being punished
when he ran away.
But this time,
he didn't even do anything!

Wally didn't walk back
to Seller Man's house.

Instead, he walked right out of town!

He wanted to find the Freedom Fighters.
He wanted to find the train.
He wanted to find a way
back to his family.

So he hid in the swamps.
A whole day passed.
And then another.

He hid and walked.
And walked and hid.

He ate berries
and melons
and whatever
he could find.

He came to a river,
and he swam across it.

He kept walking and hiding.
And the days kept passing by.

He came to another river.

This one was full of snakes
and alligators.

But he swam across that, too.

Finally, Wally ran out of land
to walk on...

The Bay lay in front of him
like a giant, blue-green blanket.

Shots rang across the water.

Gunboats.
Wally knew some of them
were from the
Freedom Fighters.

He prayed hard.

**If he could get to the Freedom Fighters...
they could help him get back to his family.**

The next morning , the tide pushed
a little boat onto the shore.

It was as beat up as Wally T,
but
a thing need not be perfect
to be useful.

Wally found a big stick,
climbed into the boat,
and pushed himself
out into the blue-green water.

Giant waves rocked the little boat,
pulling Wally far from the shore.

Just as the little boat was about to topple over...
FREEDOM floated right up to it!

"Jump in!”
“Jump in!"

Wally could hear voices.

"JUUUMP IIIIIINN!!!"

He jumped
just as a giant wave
tipped his little boat
right over.

Wally landed in the gunboat with a thud.

They were shocked to see him.
He was shocked to see them.
They were young just like Wally T.

Real live FREEDOM FIGHTERS!!!

They gave Wally
some food
and some dry clothes.

They let him sleep in
one of their tents.

The next day, they took
him to meet the Big Boss.

He asked Wally all
about the town
where the Seller Man lived.

The Freedom Fighters wanted to take over the whole town!

Wally told everything he knew.

The Big Boss told Wally
that he could stay
and help the Freedom Fighters
until the war was over.

So he stayed.

He was with them
when they went and took over the town
AS A FREE MAN!

As soon as the war was over...
and all the HARDWORKING PEOPLE
were FREE...

Wally T went back
to the small farm.
And he found Miss Courtney
and his brothers and sisters.

They all went to live in a new place
together.
And he never left them again.

This was the story of
Wally T.
It took him five tries
But he made himself FREE.

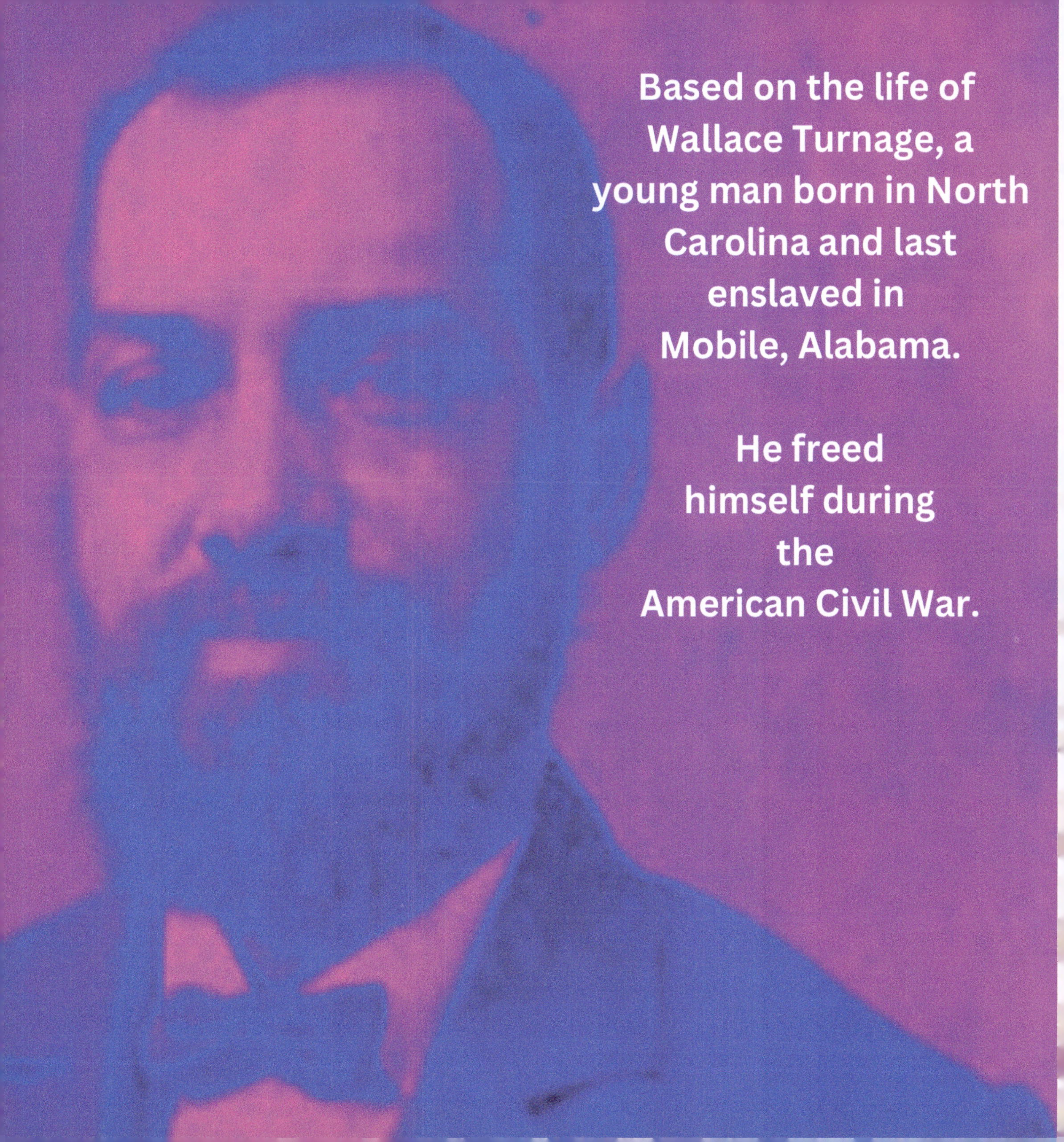

Based on the life of
Wallace Turnage, a
young man born in North
Carolina and last
enslaved in
Mobile, Alabama.

He freed
himself during
the
American Civil War.

About the Illustrator

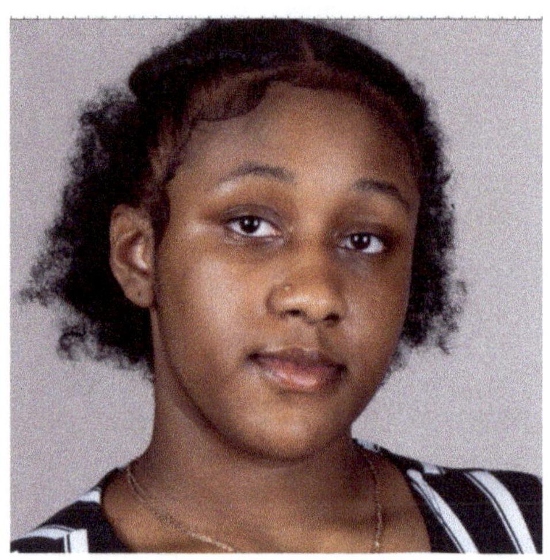

Janaiyah Baldwin is a student at Booker T. Washington Magnet High School in Montgomery, AL. She is a native of the Bronx, New York and moved to Alabama at age 12.

She is currently studying Photography, and is also an adamant visual artist. "I like to do a little bit of everything." She also enjoys creating skin care products and is currently launching a business to sell exfoliating scrubs.

Janaiyah plans to study Psychology in college and to continue as an entrepreneur when she enters politics at an early age. She intends to run for mayor of Montgomery, and ultimately aspires to be President of the United States.

About the Editor

Justice Ray is a student at Vista Peak High School in her hometown of Aurora, Colorado. Justice has many interests from science to fashion. She has a love for sports especially basketball and track.

Along with participating in athletics, Justice enjoys posting on social media. She hopes to one day be a popular content creator who inspires others to be true to themselves. Justice likes exploring streetwear fashion and is working on building her own style

After high school Justice will combine her interests in sports and science. She will attend college to study to be an athletic trainer for the NBA, getting her start in sports medicine and biomedical classes.

About the Author

Simone is a Colorado native and an alumna of Tuskegee University. She holds graduate degrees from Saint Xavier University in Chicago and the University of Memphis. Simone is the mother of two adult children, Amani and Ramon, and one granddaughter, Aniya Simone. She has worked in Education since 1997.

Simone's was first published in the *Agnieska's Dowry* collection in 1997. She has since written for local publications in Chicago and Memphis and edited multiple fiction and nonfiction works.

In 2016, Simone created the **Unheard Of** imprint to highlight the often overlooked contributions of Black Americans. She has authored three **Unheard Of** books for young readers: *365 Days of Black Men in History* (2016), *Father of the Movement: Vernon Johns* (2020) and *Driven: A 107 Year Fight for Equality* (2022).

www.ingramcontent.com/pod-product-compliance
Lightning Source LLC
Chambersburg PA
CBHW040154110726
48005CB00018B/2757